IMPERMANENT WAYS SP_____

Midland & South Western Junction Railway

Part 2

Kevin Robertson
www.crecy.co.uk

First published in 2018 by Crécy Publishing

ISBN 978 1 909328 81 5

A CIP record for this book is available from the British Library

Printed in England by LatimerTrend

www.crecy.co.uk

Front cover The end of the MSWJ. A 'Hymek' diesel stands on the one remaining siding at Savernake West that was once part of the route to Swindon. In the foreground the main West of England line runs east to west whilst in the background is the earthworks of the former Marlborough & Grafton line. The diesel was likely there awaiting an engineer's duty. *Sean Bolan*

Frontispiece The final weekend of public traffic on the line is represented here by Saturday 9 September 1961, and the day's trains were fortunately covered well by contemporary photographers. We start with this view of a quiet Saturday at Swindon Town, where a somewhat grimy pannier tank is setting off light engine towards Rushey Platt watched by just a man and a child. This scene was sadly so typical, in that it showed a railway that had simply fallen out of use, its time having passed, and was one that had already been repeated at countless locations elsewhere — not just on the MSWJ. *Amyas Crump collection*

Rear cover No 7808 *Cookham Manor* pauses at Cricklade on the down run for one of the obligatory photo stops. By this time no one seemed to mind too much about a bit of trespass, especially as nothing was due on the up line – it was a case of alight whichever side you wish. No doubt all those travelling would have been summoned back to the train with judicious whistling when it came to departure. After this date, the section of line from Swindon north through Cricklade to Cirencester would remain open for freight. *Alan Jarvis*

Below Unfortunately the gremlins had a bite at Part 1 and the following view which should have appeared around page 95 was omitted. It shows, Jim Hunt and 'Jim' Flippance with a hand-propelled permanent way trolley believed to be on the up line at Grafton South opposite the signal box. Regardless of the location, and assuming this is a running line and not a siding, the men would have obtained the permission of the signalmen controlling the section of line before placing their trolley on the line. The structure behind could well be a lamp hut. *Gwenda Ellison*

CONTENTS

INTRODUCTION

When I commenced this pictorial journey of the former Midland & South Western Junction Railway I had little idea where it would actually lead. Practically, from Cheltenham through to Andover of course, but more specifically I had no idea as to the amount of material that would be placed at my disposal.

Having instigated (at the suggestion of Jeffery Grayer) the 'Impermanent Ways' series when I was running Noodle Books, the remit then set was very specific – closed views and geographical counties only. This theme was religiously followed for some years until I was asked the obvious: 'Why do you not include some views of the railways featured when they were in operation?' If that was what was required, then so be it, an added bonus being that it was becoming increasingly difficult to locate sufficient 'closed' views for specific counties.

With Crecy Publishing having taken over Noodle Books in 2016, it was decided to develop the series further and include not just a selection of 'operational' views but also to consider books specific to one particular line. Hence 'Impermanent Ways: Midland & South Western Junction Railway', while in addition increasing the page count slightly to produce 'Special Issues' where appropriate.

Here, though, we have taken things even further, the amount of material presented meaning that a single volume would not be enough even in enlarged form. Thus with the availability of so much colour I am grateful to Crecy for allowing me the indulgence of a 'Part 1' and a 'Part 2' on the same topic.

To make sense of what follows the reader is assumed to already have 'Part1' (shame on you if you have missed it so far!). In Part 1 you will find the story that led up to the last trains, in other words the construction, operation and subsequent run-down of the railway together with the closures and economies that had taken place prior to 1961.

The two books should therefore be seen as a single work. My only wish is that they give the reader a sense of nostalgia for what had gone before.

Kevin Robertson

ABBREVIATIONS

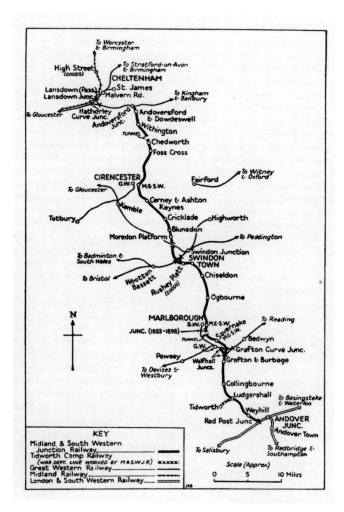

A&R – Andover & Redbridge Railway
B&C – Banbury & Cheltenham Railway
B&H – Berks & Hants Railway
B&HER – Berks & Hants Extension Railway
DEMU – Diesel-electric multiple unit
DNS – Didcot, Newbury & Southampton Railway
ESM – Economic System of Maintenance
GWR – Great Western Railway
LSWR – London & South Western Railway
MESM – Motor Economic System of Maintenance
Mid R – Midland Railway
MRly – Marlborough Railway
M&G – Marlborough & Grafton Railway
PT – pannier tank
RCH – Railway Clearing House
SCE – Swindon & Cheltenham Extension Railway
SMA – Swindon, Marlborough & Andover Railway
S&D – Somerset & Dorset Railway

Note – The generic word 'token' has been used in the text to refer to single-line working. This should be seen as referring to 'tablet', 'staff', or 'token' types, all of which effect the same result.

PART 3 – SPOTLIGHT: THE FINAL WEEKEND, 9/10 SEPTEMBER 1961

Last-day trains at Chiseldon. Pannier tank No 4697 stands at the platform with a short working, likely from Andover or Savernake to Swindon. With the curved platform, the driver has of necessity to lean some way out of the cab to watch for the guard's flag when he is ready. Notice the gas lamp, old-fashioned technology that was in use until the very end. *Mark B. Warburton, courtesy of Mrs Margaret Warburton*

A process that had occurred hundreds, nay thousands, of times over the years: the ritual of the token exchange. It is seen here being carried out on one of the last occasions with the train almost ready to leave on what was a wonderfully warm September afternoon. *Mark B. Warburton, courtesy of Mrs Margaret Warburton*

And finally the train departs. One might perhaps wonder what was in the minds of those seen on the platform who had witnessed the event. *Mark B. Warburton, courtesy of Mrs Margaret Warburton*

Both pages On the same day, 9 September 1961, another beautifully clean ex-works steam engine, '63xx' No 6395, is seen on the up line at Marlborough with 'Lomac'-type vehicles likely to have originated from Ludgershall or Tidworth (Tidworth was still open for military use at this time). The engine is seen in the platform, then being signalled away north. No 6395 would also feature in the final-day specials on 10 September. Note that the top of the water filler on the tender has been left open. In the background is a passenger train, possibly another 'short' working waiting to enter the down platform. *Mark B. Warburton, courtesy of Mrs Margaret Warburton*

Both pages The local service has now entered the bay at Marlborough and will shortly set off, destined just for Savernake. Since 1958 the timetable had been 'adjusted' so as to provide more in the way of local workings and, as has already been mentioned, very limited opportunity in the form of through trains. Sadly we may wonder exactly how much custom would have been generated by a simple Marlborough to Savernake shuttle (see the next sequence)? Notwithstanding that this was indeed the last day of public working, there is a distinct lack of obvious camera-wielding enthusiasts to record the occasion. Perhaps they were all waiting for the following day's special trains. *Mark B. Warburton, courtesy of Mrs Margaret Warburton*

Both pages Photographer Mark Warburton evidently drove to Savernake rather than using the train, and there he recorded 'U' No 31791 arriving from the direction of Swindon probably at the head of the daily through train from Cheltenham. (Just a few years earlier in 1954 there had been three such though workings daily.) Assuming that to be the case, this would have been the very last public working over the length of the line. At least one other interested spectator is visible on the road bridge, but again no one is obvious on the platforms.

Next we see No 5570 again, entering the bay platform at Savernake (Low Level). Unfortunately Mark did not record the full shunt and run-round move necessary to get the locomotive attached to the opposite end ready for the return run, although we do see the shunter riding on the footsteps of the engine as the train is propelled back into the bay. A few more observers are also present ready for the departure. Notice too that the former backing signal out of the bay has been replaced by a more modern elevated disc.

In the final view, with the train waiting to depart, the course of the branch can be made out curving away to the right. In the background the route of the former M&G can be identified by the scar across the grassland; by this time it was totally out of use. *Mark B. Warburton, courtesy of Mrs Margaret Warburton*

Two special trains ran on the final day, Sunday 10 September. The first was the Stephenson Locomotive Society (Midland Area) 'Farewell to the MSWJ railtour' behind No 7808 *Cookham Manor*. Departure was scheduled for 9.40am from Birmingham Snow Hill with a scheduled return of 8.55pm. On the outward journey the train reached Cheltenham Malvern Road having travelled via Stratford-upon-Avon, after which the route was via Swindon Town, where participants could either alight for an a tour of Swindon Works or continue south to travel the complete route of the line. After turning the engine at Ludgershall on the way back from Andover, the tour repeated the same route back, collecting any participants who had opted to look around the works. A rake of modern Mark 1 coaches was used, and certainly from photographs the train appeared well patronised.

The second special train was sponsored by the London branch of the Railway Correspondence & Travel Society and utilised No 5306 on a train of eight coaches. This, however, started at Swindon, those from London making their way by a scheduled service from Paddington. From Swindon Junction station the route was via Rushey Platt to Swindon Town, and thence south to Andover Junction, where No 5306 was turned ready for the return working, which traversed the complete route of the MSWJ to terminate at Cheltenham. Here there was a reversal, with the final leg of the journey via Stroud to Swindon. The timings for this tour were departing Swindon at 11.50am, with a scheduled return of 6.30pm. The two services crossed at Ludgershall, the SLS service with No 7808 being held to await No 5306, which was heading north. The RCTS service did not stop at Ludgershall and the passengers of both trains therefore had no time to compare notes.

Below Easy work for No 31816 just past Grafton South Junction – seen in the background – as it nears Wolfhall Junction with an up train. Grafton South Junction had lost much of its importance by this time, with the line to Grafton East closed and likewise the through route over the M&G. Notice the farm workers in the field. *Mark B. Warburton, courtesy of Mrs Margaret Warburton*

This page Before illustrating the special working, this particular view is a bit of a puzzler. Seen at Swindon Town on Sunday 10 September, intermingled with the special workings, was the limited public Sunday service. This first view shows No 6395 on an ordinary passenger train waiting to head south. The second image is again of No 6395 and an unidentified sister engine entering Marlborough from the south. Four coaches make up the formation, including what appears to be at the front (for the up train) a former Great Northern Railway brake. Four coaches and two engines would cause little difficulty for the pair. The working is clearly attracting the attention of the photographers on what was not as good a day for weather as the day before. The puzzle has to be the use of the GNR coach; was this simply an opportunity to clear stock – and perhaps an engine – from Andover? No 6395 had also been seen the previous day on freight at Andover. Notice in the background of the Marlborough view that the roof of the former High Level station is starting to deteriorate. *Unknown/Alan Jarvis*

No 7808 *Cookham Manor* pauses at Cricklade on the down run for one of the obligatory photo stops. By this time no one seemed to mind too much about a bit of trespass, especially as nothing was due on the up line – it was a case of alight whichever side you wish. No doubt all those travelling would have been summoned back to the train with judicious whistling when it came to departure. After this date, the section of line from Swindon north through Cricklade to Cirencester would remain open for freight.
Alan Jarvis

No 7808 has steam to spare at Swindon Town on the way south. Notice the white painted buffers and 'A' Class headcode, together with the train identification 'X06', the letter 'X' referring to a special working. In the background the former MSWJ offices – known as 'The Croft' - almost appear to be looking down on proceedings. *Amyas Crump collection*

The special has now reached Marlborough, and pulled up for the first time. As can be seen, the train of eight coaches was too long for the platform so, after stopping first in the conventional position, the engine pulled forward to allow the passengers in the remaining coaches to alight at the platform. Sadly, as was often the case with special workings, the number of passengers seen exceeded the normal number several-fold. The platform running-in nameboard is faded, as well might be expected, but also carries no reference to 'Low Level'. *Alan Jarvis*

The train has now pulled forward and is past the starting signal, which is still 'on'. Notwithstanding that this was a special working (and likely nothing was due on the up line), permission from the signalman would still have been required before this movement could have been undertaken. I'm not sure how well the washing would have dried in the station cottage garden on the day! *Mark B. Warburton, courtesy of Mrs Margaret Warburton*

The special is now waiting at Ludgershall, which was of course where the southbound service met the northbound RCTS train. The weather appears also to have improved, while the expanse of the platforms described earlier can also be seen to best effect. *Mark B. Warburton, courtesy of Mrs Margaret Warburton*

The two special services crossed each other at Ludgershall, and No 5306 with the RCTS train ran straight through northbound non-stop. From Ludgershall south the line through Weyhill had reverted to single line in August 1960. Beyond No 7808, the starting signal for the down train is a Great Western arm on a concrete GWR post, a relic going back to post-Grouping days. Notice too the fireman taking the opportunity to move some coal forward, while the crew have also joined into the spirit of the occasion with some visitors invited on to the footplate – as indeed we shall see more of later. *Alan Jarvis*

The special approaches Red Post Junction with the up home signal in the 'off' position further back, although this applied to the up West of England main line. From August 1960 onwards the connection at the south end of the MSWJ was made at Andover Junction, and Red Post Junction signal box played no part in controlling trains on the line; the MSWJ continuing as a separate line for the remaining distance to Andover. *Tony Molyneaux*

Finally we arrive at Andover where No 7808 is seen waiting to be uncoupled. The turntable here could not accommodate an engine the length of the 'Manor', so it was run round and coupled to the other end of the train to run tender-first back to Ludgershall, where use was made of the turntable there. On the up through line Southern 'S15' No 30828 passes with an up van train. *Alan Jarvis*

Tender-first running for No 7808 at Red Post Junction. *Tony Molyneaux*

Having turned at Ludgershall, No 7808 returns to its train with a few unofficial passengers – the one on the front framing was a brave man. *Mark B. Warburton, courtesy of Mrs Margaret Warburton*

Recoupled and ready for the off. In the foreground is the former bay platform once used by trains to Tidworth. *Mark B. Warburton, courtesy of Mrs Margaret Warburton*

Perhaps no one had told British Railways that the information was six years out of date when photographed on 10 September 1961. *Alan Jarvis*

The train pauses at Rushey Platt while necessary conversation takes place: the local football team, the state of the brassicas, the running of this service, or perhaps even what each man would be doing the next day. The colour scheme of the signal box would appear to be chocolate and a cream that has faded almost to white. *Mark B. Warburton, courtesy of Mrs Margaret Warburton*

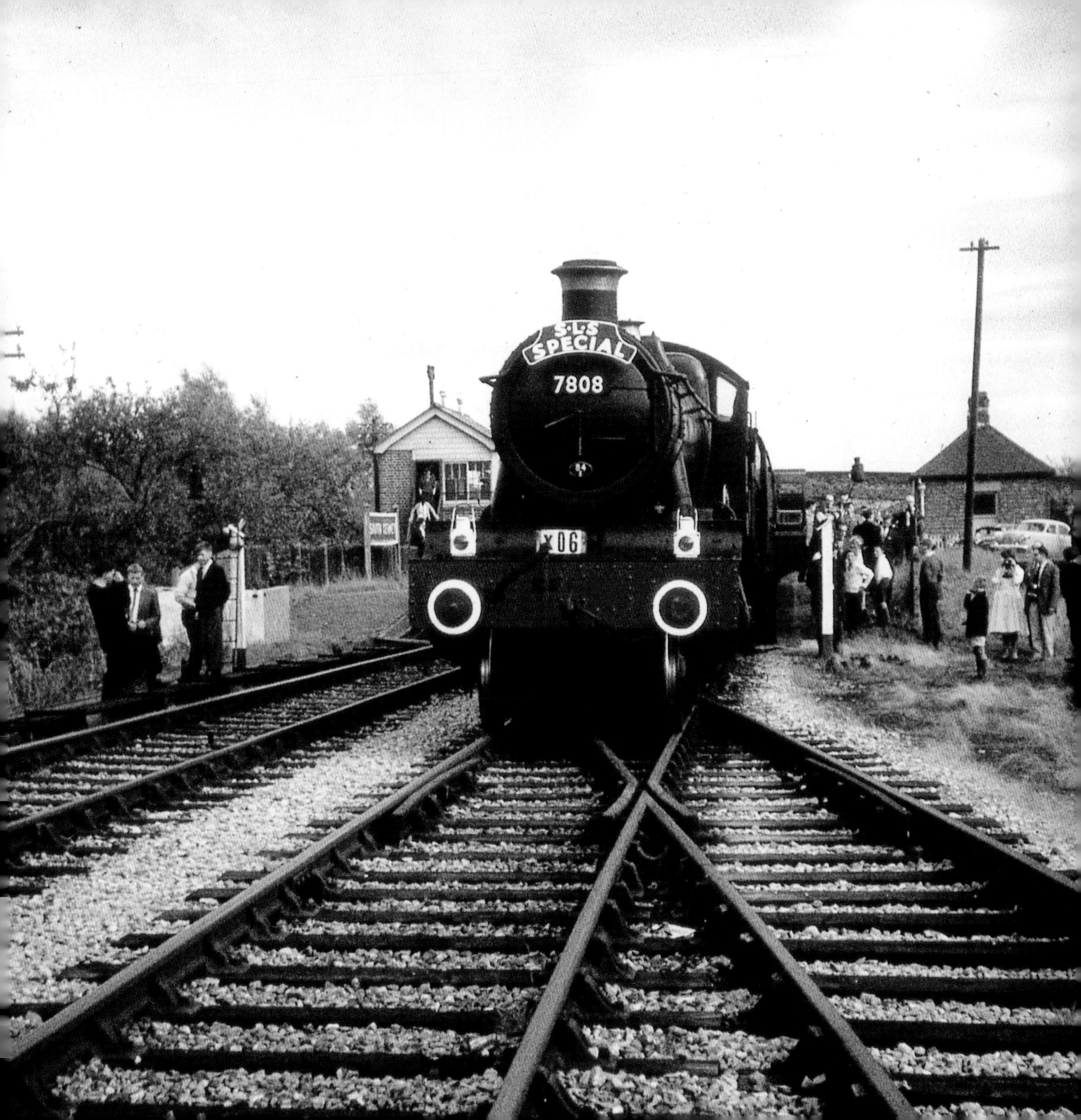
S·L·S
SPECIAL
7808
X06

Both pages The final views of the SLS special are at South Cerney, which was likely also the final photographic stop. As this special had followed the RCTS train south, those on board were indeed the last fare-paying passengers to travel the length of the MSWJ. Evidently visits to the signal boxes were also permitted! Notice also the loco inspector on the footplate with his badge of office – the bowler hat.

We now turn to the RCTS tour. Unfortunately no views of the train heading south have been found, but here is the train passing Red Post Junction and travelling north on the former MSWJ down line; the former MSWJ up line is immediately to the right of the train. The other two running lines are the LSWR main line to the West. Although the signals applicable to the MSWJ route have been removed, Red Post Junction signal box was still very much active for main-line trains. *Tony Molyneaux*

The same train is seen again approaching Ludgershall. The gross weight of the service was 285 tons, a not inconsiderable load for the engine over what was not necessarily an easy line. However, No 5306 performed admirably, being in excellent condition outside – and in. *Mark B. Warburton, courtesy of Mrs Margaret Warburton*

Left In poor light a stop was made at Swindon Town prior to heading north. It is the horn from the arm of the set-down post for the single-line section from Rushey Platt that appears in the left of the picture. *Amyas Crump collection*

Below left To Cirencester now, a sad reflection of its once grandiose state as locomotive headquarters of the MSWJ. As commented earlier, the former up line had of necessity to be taken out of use due to bridge damage and all trains were now using the down line. Mrs Margaret Warburton, whose husband Mark's images feature heavily in both volumes, recalls her own memories of the line. "I was at school at Cirencester during WW2 and watched the long hospital trains along the other side of the playing fields. (I would sit on a pile of text books to be able to see out of the windows.) Earlier I travelled on the line from Cricklade to Ludgershall and thence to Tidworth where my uncle was the station clerk cum dogsbody. *Amyas Crump collection*

This final view of the 10 September specials sees No 5306 at Foss Cross. It would appear to have also been the final photo stop of the journey – on the MSWJ at least. In future there would be further trains as far north as Cirencester and indeed specials to Ludgershall and Marlborough, as well as goods workings. After this date, however – unless there was need to clear any wagons from the respective yards from Andoversford as far south as here – the next time there would be any movement along these rails would be the sound of a demolition train. *Amyas Crump collection*

PART 4 – A SAD REFLECTION

Before we look at the MSWJ prior to the commencement of major demolition, here is a brief flashback to a different type of demolition, represented here by the last of the former MSWJ engines, No 10 (GWR No 1334), which together with sister engine No 1335 had been withdrawn in September 1952, both with 60 years of service. Now unloved and unwanted, its last years had been spent either plying the Lambourn branch or on local workings around Didcot and Reading. Now it stands in the yard of 'C' Shop at Swindon already devoid of its tender and awaiting one final move – to the cutting shed.

One of the necessary tasks undertaken following the closure of the railway was the recovery of any material that might be considered reusable. Items in this category would include any railway vehicles that had been left in a goods yard – unless the location was to retain its goods facilities – or the safe from a station booking office, while unused supplies of tickets would be consigned to the audit office at Paddington. Sometimes specific items of signalling might also be recovered, but otherwise it was a simple question of letting nature, and indeed time, take its course. This is Ogbourne in October 1961, a month after closure. So far little has been touched, with the signal box seemingly switched out of circuit as the up starting signal in the distance is 'off', although from the rust on the rails it is clear nothing has passed for some time. On the left there is a bricked-up section to the face of the platform, which was where the point rodding and signal wires had exited from the original platform signal box. Both Ogbourne and Chiseldon had closed to all traffic with the passing of the last special trains. *Amyas Crump collection*

Left It's a similar scene at Marlborough, probably seen at around the same time. Goods was still being handled here, with four goods trains each week until they were withdrawn in May 1964. In addition there was the occasional special train for pupils at the start and end of the Marlborough College term, these operating until September 1964. All these last services operated via Savernake, with the irony that one of the very last of these college trains, diesel-hauled by now, literally 'fell off' at the north end of the station in 1964 when the driver simply ran out of track in the course of running round, the route beyond here towards Swindon having already been lifted. *Amyas Crump collection*

Left At the other end of Marlborough station the connection to the High level site is seen post-1961 – the hopper wagons are standing on the High Level lines. Even in black and white there is general air of dereliction. *Courtesy of Stephen Duffell*

The day that the train came down --

Left The one that fell off! On 1 May 1964 what was the very last Paddington to Marlborough College special (via Savernake of course) came to grief on the run-round at the station. There was a crossover behind the engine which would have been a much better option! *The Marlborough Times via Richard James*

Below Elsewhere things might appear to have changed little. A Banbury-bound train is seen entering Andoversford on the line from Cheltenham to Banbury in October 1962. However, that same month would witness the end of passenger services through the station, although freight would linger a little longer. *Amyas Crump collection*

Left Closure of the MSWJ as a through route still resulted in certain sections retaining a freight service, at least for some time. These were between Swindon and Cirencester, Savernake and Marlborough, and Andover to Ludgershall. In addition, there remained a morning and evening passenger service for workmen between Cirencester and Swindon and return. This was a concession to the former MSWJ staff when the works at Cirencester had closed soon after 1923 and men were transferred to the GWR works at Swindon. The railway company promised to continue to operate the service as long as there at least three workmen using it daily. Such a train is seen here arriving at Cirencester in the last days of operation, with No 3780 in charge of the afternoon return working. *Courtesy of Stephen Duffell*

Left Here the same engine is seen running around its train ready for the return journey. A further run-round was required at Swindon Town in each direction. *Courtesy of Stephen Duffell*

Right Freight services continued to operate between Swindon and Cirencester until 1 April 1964, although the intermediate locations of Cerney & Ashton Keynes and Cricklade had lost their freight services the previous year. As time passed these workings were often diesel-hauled, although around the same time '38xx' 2-8-0 No 3853 was recorded shunting the yard at Cirencester. Officially this engine had been withdrawn at the end of 1963, but may well have been resurrected on a temporary basis; certainly it appears in poor external condition with a missing cover to the safety vale. *Courtesy of Stephen Duffell*

Right Might this more distant view of No 3853 with its train have been the final working clearing the yard of any remaining wagons? Some coal traffic would remain between Swindon and Moredon for the power station, although the line was closed north of the 35m 20ch point from 31 March 1963. Moredon traffic would continue until about 1968/69. Notice on the right that the buildings of the former locomotive works still remain. *Courtesy of Stephen Duffell*

A brief flashback to the past when Cirencester works was active. Here we see lines of goods stock; that on the left is facing towards the single-road 'Running Repairs Shop', while the two lines on the right are facing the 'Carriage & Wagon Repairs Shop'. The building on the left, at right-angles to the railway, was part of the general store. Notice the condition of the track on the left, which was fortunately a dead-end siding, not a running line!

We are now inside what was the body-makers and paint shop in 1926, after closure by the GWR. Following takeover, the new owner had been quick to end work here, carriage and wagon work ceasing in 1924 and locomotive work in March 1925. The works officially closed in October 1925, having spent its last days as a store for brand-new engines delivered from outside builders and not yet accepted into service. Subsequently the buildings found a new use unconnected with the railway until years later, when the site was eventually cleared for road improvements.

There was also a locomotive depot at Cirencester, seen here as the backdrop to this view of No 5 seemingly being cleaned around 1920. The site also possessed a turntable. Both the shed and turntable were taken out of use by the GWR as early as March 1924. Engine No 5 was a 4-4-0 built by the North British Locomotive Company in 1912 – the MSWJ never built any locomotives itself. It was subsequently renumbered 1123 by the GWR and remained in service until March 1938.

After 1964 on the former SCE route, nature began to reclaim what had once been hers. Here is South Cerney looking south; no more will 'Galloping Alice' (as one of the former MSWJ engines was affectionately nicknamed) or her sisters pound the rails. *Courtesy of Stephen Duffell*

Left Rusting rails looking south at Rushey Platt. The signal box is long gone but the connection to and from the former GWR main line survives – indeed, it was the only means of accessing the line to Swindon Town, then the reversal to Moredon or, before that, Cirencester. Now there will be no more trains. *Peter Russell*

Left Looking north, the junction between the two lines is visible. Following removal of all signalling, points had been converted to hand operation, while the double-ended catch point may also be noted in the track arriving from the main line. The former Rushey Platt station building has also been demolished.
Peter Russell

It is surprising to relate is that the former goods yard at Rushey Platt – in reality little more than a single siding – continued to handle timber traffic until 1974. Here the expanse of the facility is visible and with the base of one of the old Rushey Platt station buildings visible on the left. *Peter Russell*

Above Looking down towards the Great Western main line, the connection from Rushey Platt is seen coming in from the right. A Class 47 diesel is at the head of a London-bound Inter-City working. In the background is the expanse of Swindon Works. *Peter Russell*

Opposite Meanwhile, slightly further south various changes were taking place at Swindon Town. It's now 1971 and the features so long recognised as part of the station have gone: the station buildings, footbridge and signal boxes. There had been two boxes, 'A' at the north end and 'B' at the south end, and both had been closed from September 1964. General goods had ceased in May 1964, although coal would linger on until November 1966. But is was to be a drawn-out demise, as oil traffic was still handled up to November 1968, after which there was a period of inactivity until the spring of 1970. This was the time the M4 motorway was being built through Wiltshire and the site of Swindon Town took on its final use as the railhead for stone used in the construction of the road. To cope with the traffic an abandoned loop siding on the west side of the station was reinstated and thousands of tons of stone arrived to be deposited on the former up platform before being taken away by road to the construction site – some can be seen on the left of the picture. There was not a little irony in this traffic, for the new road would dissect the railway south of Swindon and thus permanently sever the trackbed between here and Chiseldon.

(caption continued) The fact that this portion of the line was still in use was not lost on the enthusiast fraternity, and on 27 March 1971 the remains were visited by a three-car DMU forming the GWS/WRC 'Somerset Rambler III' railtour. (The special also visited the former Holt Junction on the Chippenham-Devizes line, Cranmore on the former Witham-Yatton branch, Merehead Quarry and Portishead on a varied itinerary.) The final passenger train reached Swindon Town on 16 April 1972 when the LCGB 'Somerset Quarryman' railtour arrived in the shape of a four-car 'Inter-City'-type DMU. The MSWJ was of course principally a steam railway, diesel traffic being confined to the two railtours referred to here and the final workings to Cirencester, together with, post-steam, the various trips to serve the Army at Ludgershall. But it should not be forgotten that in about 1960 the line from Swindon north was also used for testing, crew training and familiarisation of diesel sets built at Swindon, the MSWJ having sufficient spare capacity for this to be undertaken without interrupting regular traffic. Swindon Town would finally lose its last traffic in 1972. *Derek Fear*

Above Swindon Town is seen from the north, now totally devoid of traffic and awaiting its fate.

Opposite above The deserted railway is seen again from the opposite direction.

Opposite below This is looking south towards Marlborough. A couple of road oil-tankers are the only signs of movement, while recovered track panels await collection.

At Chiseldon decay is also the order of the day. This view was likely taken a few years earlier than those at Swindon and, while debris is a feature, most if not all of the signal box windows appear intact. Sometimes the railway would pay a retainer to a recently retired railwayman to 'keep an eye' on the site, but it would still be difficult to do this all the time. No doubt to the railwayana collector the station would have yielded rich pickings.

Above No more trains at Savernake High Level. Years earlier Sir Sam Fay had commented that it was the building of the Marlborough and Grafton line that had been the saviour of the company, yet now, less than 70 years later, its purpose is no more. *Amyas Crump collection*

Below Nature attempts to reclaim the former signal box at Savernake High Level. The structure has spent far more years out of use than operating in its original role.

It was not much better news at the former Low Level station. This closed to passengers on 18 April 1966 and was demolished soon after. Already in the background demolition can be seen to be taking place, but ironically the annotation 'For Marlborough' had continued to be displayed for almost five years from September 1961 until April 1966 – one wonders whether anyone tried it! *Sean Bolan*

Right A sad end at Low Level, which had just achieved its centenary, although whether this had been marked by any celebration at all in 1962 is not known – probably unlikely. Here the platform edges have been removed as a precursor to a more general demolition. *Sean Bolan*

Below right At ground level, this is the view looking through the bridge eastwards, with Savernake East signal box just visible in the distance. The station had stood abandoned for about two years after closure, while East box and its associated signals were taken out of use from 4 December 1968. On the main line this now resulted in some long block sections: Bedwyn to Savernake West, and in the opposite direction Savernake to Pewsey. *Sean Bolan*

Here we are looking west, with the junction signal for Marlborough also replaced. The water column, however, still survives, although unused for some time. *Sean Bolan*

Seen from the trackbed of the MSWJ at Grafton South, the train in the distance is heading west on the Berks & Hants main line. To the right the formation led to Grafton East, while to the left was the route towards both Savernake Low Level and High Level.

Above Continuing south, we pause for a moment at an almost trackless Tidworth. The main structures remain but the facilities are plainly almost disused, with just a few loaded wagons on the left. *Roger Holmes*

Below This is Ludgershall around the time of closure of the main line. The pannier tank, possibly No 4616, is shunting wagons of what appears to be general goods in the yard – the shunter/guard is in shirtsleeves further up the line. In the background are typical military Nissen huts.

No 4616 is in the process of shunting condemned wagons at Ludgershall. The electrification warning plates on the front of the engine's tanks are a bit superfluous here, but were a standard fixture at the time. This is also the first time we get a view of the bay on the down side, which had been taken out of use in August 1960 at the same time as singling of the line to Weyhill and Red Post.

Above At Ludgershall after 1961, some rationalisation has taken place on the Tidworth line but otherwise assets appear basically unchanged. What is different, though, is how the former up and down main lines to and from Collingbourne on the right have been given over to wagon storage, obviously long-term, from the state of the track. Notice that in front of each line of condemned wagons a sleeper has been placed across the track.

Below In 1962 the once busy station of Ludgershall is now almost totally surplus to requirements.

The Locomotive Club of Great Britain 'Anton and Test Valley' railtour of 6 September 1964, behind Standard Class 3 tank No 82029, is working 'wrong line' at Ludgershall. This tour visited Winchester Chesil (closed to passengers in March 1960) before running down to Southampton and thence via Romsey and Stockbridge to Ludgershall. It seems very likely that the engine was turned here, as it is known to been facing south when the tour had first left Winchester. Notice how pieces of the canopy valance have been lost in the two years since the last view. *Amyas Crump collection*

Ludgershall signal box finally closed in February 1963, signals were removed and points converted to hand operation – it is just possible to identify a point lever standing vertical between the two running lines. Before this time Peter Squibb recounts one day being called as duty lineman to what appeared to be an electrical fault in Ludgershall box. The signalman on duty had reported he was receiving spurious bells from the then closed signal box at Collingbourne – this was after 1961 when the line north of Ludgershall had closed to all traffic. Peter suspected that it might be children playing about, but nevertheless set off to investigate. What he found instead was the scrap contractors in the process of ripping out the equipment from the box and lifting the track, during which some electrical contacts had been made, causing the bells to appear to ring further south. The ghosts of past trains perhaps?
Derek Fear

One might be tempted to suggest that this was the end of Ludgershall, rationalisation certainly having occurred with the removal of the down platform, buildings, signal box and footbridge. Certainly there is less infrastructure, but the railway was still seeing traffic and indeed would continue to do so into the 21st century.

Little-used and freight-only lines were regularly visited by railway societies, often using motive power that was, to say the least, unusual. Here it is 'Britannia' Class 4-6-2 No 70020 *Mercury*, running tender-first through Weyhill on the return leg to Andover of the Southern Counties Touring Society 'South Western Rambler' tour of 8 March 1964. This trip commenced and terminated at Waterloo, taking in the stub of the MSWJ to Ludgershall before returning to the main line and continuing to Templecombe for a journey over the southern half of the Somerset & Dorset line. Behind the locomotive the chimneys of Weyhill station are visible, as well as the disused signal box on the extreme left, closed in August 1960 when the former up line was made redundant. *Tony Molyneaux*

Another steam special, this time headed by No 35023 *Holland-Afrika Line*, passes Weyhill with another Southern Counties Touring Society special, this one the 'Four Counties' tour of 9 October 1966. This trip had started at Victoria, with No 35023 taking over at Salisbury, thence to Andover – Ludgershall of course – and returning to Victoria via Reading and Redhill. Note that in the ensuing two years the up line has been recovered and the signal box demolished. *Derek Fear*

Above Come the end of steam, and with the continuing survival of the railway between Andover and Ludgershall on behalf of the Army, a further special visited the route on 25 July 1981, jointly organised by the RCTS and Southern Electric Group. A three-car DMU was used, and the tour started from Paddington, arriving at Ludgershall via Basingstoke and Andover. Later in the day the trip took in the various quarries near Merehead before seeing the stub of the Highworth branch at Swindon. The service is seen here at Ludgershall. *Amyas Crump collection*

Opposite However, steam would return, and this time not even a former GWR type. On 26 September 1987 the 'Hampshire Whistler' used former S&D 7F 2-8-0 No 53809, which was photographed running light engine through the remains of Ludgershall station while undertaking shuttle duties in connection with the tour. Two diesel locomotives, Class 37 No 37116 and Class 40 No 40122, took turn and turn about with the 7F on the service, which saw nine return journeys along the branch from Andover to Ludgershall on the one day. By this time housing had been built on much of the northern part of the site, leaving just a loop and fragments of platform remaining. The last reported railtour along the line was on 8 March 2003 when Standard Class 5 No 73096 and Class 37 diesel No 37670 crawled along the branch at a stately 15mph. By this stage the platforms were no more and new housing stood on the site of the down platform. *Jeffery Grayer*

A truncated railway: Ludgershall and the remains of the Tidworth branch are seen in more recent times. All that remains are a few sidings and all appears quiet. In the distance, above the abandoned trackbed of the line to Collingbourne on the right, the bridge carrying the A342 road over the line may be made out – it was later demolished. Further south a new bridge, but single-track only, was built near Weyhill to carry the railway over the widened 'route to the west', better known as the A303 trunk road.

Right A Ministry shunter and conversation time at the disused Perham Down signal box. With all obvious signal wire and point rodding connections removed from the box and the locking room exit bricked up, it appears that the signal box has found a new use as an office.

Below right Ministry of Defence diesel shunter No 261 heads for Tidworth with Army vehicles. A variety of small diesel locomotives have operated the railway in recent years, although in the spring of 2017 there was little sign of either rail vehicles or recent movement and, sad to relate, the line's continual survival must now be in doubt. A further 2017 visit revealed that the Tidworth line had been truncated further, with a set of buffer stops placed on the north side of the A3026 (Ludgershall to Tidworth) road prior to what had once been the level crossing at Perham Down. *Sean Bolan*

Empty sidings at Ludgershall. Traffic to this last remnant of the MSWJ is sporadic; indeed, when compiling this volume I made several trips to the Ludgershall area only to view a similar scene. (Photography in the area is perhaps not necessarily wise in these security-orientated times.) However, on my last visit the yard was again full of wagons – *long live the MSWJ!*

PART 5 - THE FINAL IGNOMINY

The final ignominy was the actual demolition of this once much-used railway. Actual dates for this are not easy to find, although it appears that the northernmost section from Andoversford south to Cirencester may well have been one of the first, followed by that from Swindon to Marlborough and also Savernake to Ludgershall. Here at Withington a grimy '28xx' is being used to shunt 'redundant assets'; it, too, is likely to be redundant within a short while.

Next it is a '43xx/53xx' seen at Foss Cross with a recovery/demolition train, with the signal box seemingly already stripped of anything useful or easily removable.

Demolition through did not always go smoothly, as witness the results of a runaway north of Cirencester on 18 May 1963. A number of wagons have managed to derail themselves, probably off the end of the rails, and a contractor's crane and small 'Planet'-type diesel are attempting to sort out the mess. *Mark B. Warburton, courtesy of Mrs Margaret Warburton*

Both pages As we have just seen, the practicalities of demolition were to have a string of flat wagons on to which sections of pre-cut track would be placed. These were then taken to a convenient point where the loaded wagon(s) would be detached and the train returned to where the crane was waiting. Here we see this operation in place near Chedworth. At the head is a contractor's diesel locomotive; Pittrail Ltd was a scrap contractor that was also involved in the demolition of at least one other former GWR line, the Chard branch, in 1965. At the rear is a Ruston Bucyrus crane. *Sean Bolan collection*

Both pages Also at Chedworth, this is the bridge that carried the railway over Queen Street, seen first adorned with Virginia creeper, and subsequently in a parlous state having to be supported. The demolition view is the removal of the retaining wall at nearby Well Hill. *Sean Bolan collection*

Left page South of Marlborough, Grafton station yard was used as a railhead for the collection of lifted track panels, seen here with the up side buildings removed and all signalling also recovered. *Sean Bolan collection*

Right page Further south, and believed to be near Ludgershall, we have a view of the work progressing, with a redundant signal in the background. Assuming that the diesel locomotive is the same one seen in the distance in the last views of Grafton, we can state that it was also the up line that was removed first. *Sean Bolan collection*

WEDNESDAY APRIL 22 1964

A railway line after the public controversy, argument or inquiry at the time of its closure is forgotten. The photograph shows the demolition work at present in progress on the closed stretch of railway between Marlborough and Swindon in Wiltshire. A mobile crane lifts a section of the track and loads it on to a wagon which is standing on the next bit of track to be lifted.

South of Swindon the demolition managed to attract the attention of *The Times* for April 1964 – perhaps it was a quiet news day! At least we also have confirmation that the same crane and therefore Messrs Pittrail were still involved. Possibly the feature was included in the newspaper as part of a wider topic covering the Dr Beeching closures, which were in full swing at that time. Even so, it must be stated that the MSWJ closed before the good Doctor came upon the scene. An interesting aside this time relating to 'journalistic licence' concerns the *Hampshire Chronicle* newspaper, which in the early autumn of 1966 published a view of the demolition of the DNS line at the former Winchester Chesil station. The caption read along the lines of: 'Demolition of the former railway from Southampton to Cheltenham'. Really?

And after the contractors have been all is again calm. This is Andoversford looking east towards the former junction with the MSWJ in January 1966. *Andrew Muckley*

The southern portal of the 494-yard Chedworth Tunnel was located in a deep cutting north of the village, as seen here in 1972. The GWR men who maintained the stretch of line through here would have received 'tunnel allowance', as the length was greater than a quarter of a mile. Without trains it is now home to bats.

This is Chedworth station, looking south, also in January 1966. *Andrew Muckley*

Opposite far left Foss Cross. *Sean Bolan collection*

Opposite left Having received an offer for the land BR were keen to accept although the irony is the proposed Marlborough by-pass was never built! *Courtesy Richard James*

Opposite below At Cirencester, looking north, even the top of the water tower has succumbed to the insatiable appetite of the scrap merchants, although for the present at least some metal, in the form of the lamp standard and canopy supports, remains. *Andrew Muckley*

Right This is the view looking south towards the remaining buildings of the works. Today the complete site has disappeared to be replaced by industry and roads.

Below At Marlborough the 'licensed' refreshment rooms survived following closure. After the war it was in the hands of Harold Trotman, who blamed Dr Beeching for the line's demise and even renamed his house 'Beeching Villa' in protest. Notice the variation in tiles on the roof of the main station.

Above Savernake still (just) provides some reminders of days past. To the left is Savernake West signal box, and to the right a 'Hymek' (Class 35) diesel-hydraulic locomotive is on the short stub of the up refuge siding. The car – a Hillman – is on the trackbed of the former GWR branch to Marlborough. Again the course of the long-closed M&G may be traced from the shallow embankment of trees. *Sean Bolan collection*

Below Here we visit Collingbourne, or more exactly the remains thereof. A demolition contract issue by the railway would specify what was included and what must be left, and it appears certain that the station canopy supports and corrugated-iron hut were specifically excluded.

Above The route of the railway in the vicinity of Collingbourne runs parallel to the main A338 road, from which sections of the trackbed are still clearly visible to the east. These include fencing, occupation bridges and a low embankment, although Collingbourne station (and Collingbourne Kingston Halt) has long disappeared.

Below An occupation bridge at Collingbourne. *Stephen Duffell*

PART 6 – A PRIVILEGED VIEW

Any views from the footplate, regardless of the railway, are a rarity, so to be able to report the finding of a number illustrating a trip on the line in its final years must be a bonus indeed. They come from the collection of Stephen Duffell and were believed to have been taken by Driver J. Pemble. However, a steam engine was never the best place from which to take photographs, so the indulgence of the reader is sought when there was perhaps a 'bad joint' just as the shutter was pressed! Please also make allowance for the odd piece of cinder or soot on the lens. To avoid obvious duplication of information from earlier, locations only are given in this section.

Left Cheltenham St James.

Above Andoversford.

Left Withington.

Above Chedworth Tunnel, north end.

Above Chedworth station.

Opposite above Foss Cross.

Opposite below Cirencester.

211

Cricklade.

Swindon Town.

Chiseldon.

G.W.R.
4237 **TO**
Chiseldon

Chiseldon Camp Halt.

Marlborough.

Marlborough Tunnel.

Above Savernake.

Right Wolfhall Junction.

Grafton.

Collingbourne.

Andover Junction.

PART 7 - MEMENTOES FROM THE PAST

Space and necessity prohibit a detailed look at the locomotives and rolling stock of the MSWJ, and anyway that subject has already been covered in the excellent books by Mike Barnsley. Similarly, with the few exceptions that follow, the route taken by trains south of Andover has likewise had to be omitted.

South of Andover MSWJ through trains traversed the Andover-Redbridge railway, paralleling the route of the River Test, for centuries renowned for its trout fishing. Here from a high vantage point between Stockbridge and Horsebridge, a three-car 'Hampshire' DEMU heads south on exactly the same course taken by through trains between Cheltenham and Southampton for more than 70 years. This diesel service would only ever have ventured as far north as Andover Junction. *Roger Holmes*

The previous image was likely taken in the early 1960s, but half a century before and close to the same spot an MSWJ through train is seen. The engine is one of the pair of 4-4-4T engines built for the MSWJ in 1897 and numbered 17 and 18. They became GWR Nos 25 and 27 respectively and lasted until 1927/29. Notice on the front framing the re-railing jack, a feature of many locomotives of the period. The MSWJ passenger locomotive livery was crimson with black lining edged with yellow.

2-6-0 No 16 'Galloping Alice' was so called due to the impression of speed that could be gained from her small driving wheels. (Who first coined the name 'Galloping Alice' is not reported, but it was an unofficial designation as no MSWJ engines ever carried names, only numbers.) This and sister engine No 14 were to be found working through goods trains, at which task they were very successful. Only No 16 passed to the GWR, becoming that company's No 24. Swindon must have thought well of the engine for in 1925 she was taken into Swindon Works and given a standard GWR boiler and a modified cab. In this form she continued to work until 1930. One aside quoted by the RCTS is that in her latter days she was used almost exclusively on pick-up freight duties over the Badminton line between Swindon and Stoke Gifford yard. On one such occasion, following an engine failure somewhere along the route, she was unexpectedly given the task of taking over a Bristol express from a 'King' Class engine, which she successfully hauled as far as Swindon, probably living up her to nickname one final time.

This is MSWJ No 11, later GWR No 1335, but seen here in probable original condition. It was one of the three Dubs-built 2-4-0 tender engines that survived into British Railways days, and have been seen earlier. A maker's plate is on the leading splashier, with the MSWJ numberplate on the cabside and company scroll on the tender.

A final locomotive view. The 0-4-4T type was common on many railways around the latter part of the 19th century (not the GWR, however), and the MSWJ was no exception. No 15 had been built by Beyer Peacock in 1895 and would become GWR No 23. Following the Grouping No 23 remained working in the Swindon-Marlborough-Savernake area and also spent some time on the reinstated shuttle service between the two stations at Swindon.

Road competition in the 1950s resulted in people migrating away from rail to road, either using a bus or their own personal transport, and both were the cause of declining passenger revenue for the railway. That and a management that took the view that existing through freight services could be accommodated elsewhere would spell the end of the MSWJ. To sanction such actions, services were altered in 1958 so as to be 'inconvenient' to many, and the result was inevitable. It was a dark time so far as British Railways was concerned, while it must be said that the MSWJ was hardly alone in suffering such a fate. This is the scene at Andover Town in about 1960, with road traffic held up at the level crossing gates, perhaps waiting for a Cheltenham train to pass. The desire by councils to reduce road congestion also meant that pressure was exerted on the railways to remove such hold-ups. A simple answer for the time was to close the railway and thus do away with the level crossing...

Above Wistful thinking, perhaps, on the remains of the railway near Chedworth.

Left Closure notice.

Destroying the evidence: the filling-in of what had been school cutting at Chedworth. *Sean Bolan*

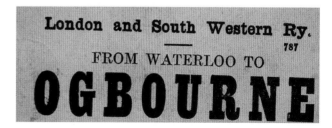

Relics now with no practical use: directors' (medallion) passes for the MSWJ route.

INDEX TO BOTH PARTS

Entries to this part marked in bold